My Search for Gregory Bell aka Norman MacCaud:
Clues in the News

Karen E. Black, MLS

My Search for Gregory Bell aka Norman MacCaud:
Clues in the News

Karen E. Black

Viceroy Power Press

ISBN: 978-0-9879866-5-8

Published by Viceroy Power Press

Please address any comments to karen.black@sympatico.ca

My Search for Gregory Bell aka Norman MacCaud: Clues in the News

Gregory Bell, whoever he really was, had no trouble finding me. I wasn't going any place. In 1993, I was a 41-year-old research librarian, the mother of five children (aged 1 to 16) and the grieving cousin of Brian Beaucage (1948-1991).

Gregory Bell found me because while he was living in Ireland under yet another assumed name, he'd also written and published a book.

He was my cousin Brian Beaucage's friend, but I didn't know this when I picked up a used copy of his novel *Birdsong* with the bloodied prisoner on its cover and read this pitch:

"Dangerous men with nothing to lose...hell erupts in a Canadian prison..."

But I immediately knew this was a fictionalized account of the 1971 Kingston Penitentiary Riot that my cousin Brian had played a key role in. I had researched the riot since I was an undergrad student at the University of Western Ontario, focusing on the only material available to me:

- various newspaper stories covering the Kingston Penitentiary Riot, April 14-18, 1971;
- my cousin Brian Beaucage's November 1971 account;
- J.W. Swackamer's *Report of the Commission of Inquiry into Certain Disturbances at Kingston Penitentiary during April 1971*
- the court transcript of the trial of 13 men, beginning October 28, 1973:
- jailhouse author Roger Caron's 1985 book, *Bingo! Four Days in Hell.*

I loved poetry and fiction, so a penitentiary uprising — even one resulting in the deaths of two inmates — wouldn't have interested me much, except that in addition to being an inmate at the time of the riot, my cousin Brian Beaucage was charged with second degree murder.

Brian had got 'off' on a reduced charge of assault in November 1972, but when he was murdered in 1991, many people still believed he was guilty.

When I read Bell's *Birdsong*, I couldn't help but compare it to another jailhouse account of the same riot: Roger Caron's *Bingo! Four Days in Hell.*

Bingo! was Caron's second book. No doubt he had been under some pressure to write it — his first book *Go Boy! Memories of a Life Behind Bars* had won the Governor General's Award in 1978.

Both books had been published years after the 1971 riot, Bell's in 1983 and Caron's in 1985. Bell's book had been marketed as a novel and Caron's as a memoir, but except for the names of the characters, the story they told was much the same.

Eight hundred inmates had launched one of the most violent riots in Canadian penal history. Living quarters were demolished, six guards were taken hostage and on the final day when the army was threatening to move in, two inmates were killed.

On a positive note, the guard-hostages were released unharmed and the prisoners issued formal grievances to the media including lack of recreational time, lack of work, and concerns about their future conditions in the newly built Millhaven Prison.

As keen observers and articulate reporters of these events, both Gregory Bell and Roger Caron assigned themselves low-key roles and kept their hands clean. By all accounts, they had done their best to protect the hostages and steer the riot to a safe conclusion without selling out their friends.

Though Caron's book was supposed to be a factual account and Bell's had been marketed as a novel, several of the key players in *Birdsong* were still recognizable.

The key participants in the riot emerged as these men:

Rebels	Roger Caron's *Bingo!*	Gregory Bell's *Birdsong*
Narrator	Roger Caron, #2 cell, Block B	Dandy Maclean
Narrator's side-kicks	Step-Ladder, Do-Die and January Jones were part of Caron's "merry band of outlaws" whose worst crimes were busting the locks to some cells[i]	
Hero	Barrie Mackenzie -B block head honcho -man who "saved the riot" after he replaced Billy Knight on Inmate Committee	Meredith 'Merry'Thomas: -B block head honcho -bank robber -sergeant in Korean War -frees his friend El Tigre -negotiates for peaceful end
Hero's friends	Norm McCaud, 38, counterfeiter, long-term prisoner; Brian Beaucage	Dandy Mclean; El Tigre
Antagonist	William "Billy"	Emmanuel Strain

	James Knight, 28 -prison barber -grew up in group homes -embittered -looked like Charlie Manson when he grew a beard -adept at disguise -jumpstarts riot and kidnaps guards -initially has custody of guard-hostages -his actions figuratively kill the hero -gets away with everything	"Manny the Maniac" -troll like appearance -obnoxious, but intelligent or "cunning" - jumpstarts riot and kidnaps guards -like a street corner preacher -led assault on two inmates who were killed -kills the hero -gets away with everything
Antagonist's friends/soldiers	Brian Dodge, Robert Adams, Allan Lafrenier, Leo Barrieault, Charles Saunders	Gopher and Axe, both long-termers
Antagonist's #2 friend		Axe-Manny sidekick #2 -both long-termers
Regional Director Warden	John Moloney, former guard Arthur Jarvis	
Boxers and/or Inmate Police Force	1. Big Wayne Ford -bald, 280 pounds, serving life time for murder; an intellectual 'gentle giant' -smashed lock on service duct to herd hostages inside for protection 2. Teddy Woods 3. Cyril Rousseau, ex-boxer	Jonathan Paterson 'El Tigre' -well-read -180 pounds -massive shoulders -tried to stop Maniac from grabbing keys -similar background to Joe Christmas's in Faulkner's *A Light in August*

Other pro boxers		Dicey Allen and Smelly Roberts
Birdman		Tommy Ryan
Small-time crooks	Oag brothers/Hal and Al Elliot ? David Shepley and his friends Ziggy and John McBride. In Caron's version, it's Shepley (and his friend Brian Beaucage who lead the assault on the 'undesirables'	John and Martin Harris; Peter Williams and Barney Ellis
Guard who lost hat when riot started	Terry Decker	Young
Other guards	Head keeper Ed Barret, 57; Donald Floyd, 45; Douglas Dittrich, 41; Joseph Valliere, 47 and Kerry Bushell, 24.	Deputy Head Keeper Cogan, Drummond, Wilson ,Macken, Jones
Mafia cook		Luigi Martinelli
		Fartin Martin
Big, illiterate Newfie		Rancid Roger
The Queens		Big Nancy, Little Violet and Francine
Hospital con	Ralph Lundrigen	Footy Morrison
News reporter Kingston radio station; TV reporter from Toronto	Jerry Retzer -got the news out Henry Champ -toured scene	Harry Fitzpatrick
Citizens' Committee members: 1. Local law professor; 2. Newspaper columnist; 3. Barrie/Merry's lawyer; 4. solicitor;	1.J. Desmond Morton (Caron's lawyer); 2. Ron Haggart; 3. Aubrey E. Golden; 4. Emmanuel Greenberg	1. Dr. Emmett Johnstone; 2. Herbert Yonge; 3. J. Firbank Haughton; 4. Peter Barrington; 5. Thomas Pringle

5. governor's cousin, local man with store down the street		
Inmate Committee members: 1. mute; 2. Enemy/Hero; 3. birdman; 4. Narrator; extras	1. ___; 2 Billy Knight/Barrie Mackenzie; 3.___; 4.Norm McCaud; 5. Ralph Lundrigen, male nurse Arthur Martin? William R. Donkin?	1.Alphonse Gaulle; 2. Merry Thomas; 3. Tommy Ryan; 4. Dandy Maclean; 5. Uncle Joe
Victims	Bertrand Robert (same crimes as Du Quesne) and the Camel (same crimes as Barney Duff) were two of 14 men tied up in dome area. Ralph Lake was another rapist who risked assault. Caron described him as Brian Beaucage's 'arch enemy' and a man disliked by most of his fellow convicts, but he was protected by bookie Harold St. Amour. James Ball was also assaulted while still in the protection unit by two unidentified convicts. Billy Knight enlisted Barrie Mackenzie and Brian Beaucage's reluctant support and "kept the wolves at bay."[ii]	Du Quesne, the baby killer who had disciplined them by sitting them on a hot stove (tortured and killed in inquisition led by pipe-wielding Manny the Maniac); Barney Duff, the pedophile (hung by Manny's orders)

There were several uncomplimentary passages about my cousin Brian Beaucage in Caron's book, but none in Bell's.

So now I had several problems. Why did the accounts differ so much? How accurate were they? And who was Gregory Bell?

I had culled the names of several of the key figures in the riot, but Bell's wasn't one of them. Maybe he'd just been a keen observer, but I didn't think so. He had written his book from a con's perspective. I checked biographical dictionaries and wrote letters to libraries and publishers, with no results. I found no Canadian reviews of *Birdsong*, nothing about the author, and in response to my query, the book's publisher, Robert Hale Ltd. of London wrote:

> Dear Madam: Thank you for your letter of March 14, 2002.
> We are sorry to say we cannot be of assistance to you as Gregory
> Bell whose real name was we think Wilfred McNeilly, died some
> time ago.

When I found out Wilfred McNeilly died before Bell's book was published in 1983, I went back to *Birdsong* for further clues. The book's first-person narrator was an inmate called Dandy Maclean, so I focused on him:

- Dandy claimed to have been born on a little Scottish island, though his family moved to Glasgow "where there was work and money and sooty misery of life;"
- Dandy was quartered in B block in the infamous Kingston Penitentiary by his own choice, a silent block of long serving men, the lowest man on the totem pole, but they all stuck together;
- Dandy worked in the library which was a good number, as good as the Joint could provide," and he had once worked in the print shop, the same place where his book's hero, Meredith "Merry" Thomas, now worked;

- Dandy, who had also worked in the editorial department of an unidentified Canadian newspaper, smelled a story before the riot even broke out: "My dormant reporting instincts came to the surface: the threat of bloody riot broods over the 130 year old mass of the penitentiary tonight as the Warden resists inmate pressure for reform..." On April 13, 1971, hours before the real riot erupted, he added these notes: This prison is a time bomb. The fuse has been lit and is burning slowly towards the detonator. Flashpoint is only a tiny fraction of time away. And nobody cares... overheated prose (Dandy editorialized), but it was an overheated situation;"
- Dandy had been so described by a judge as "the mastermind behind an international crime syndicate" and handed down the fourteen years (he) could only gape at him and stammer: "But it's a first offence. That's a bit steep for a first offence;"
- Dandy served as secretary on the Inmate Committee, a group of four to six people, who negotiated with the outside world during the riot;
- Dandy spent most of his time with fellow prisoner Merry Thomas (aka Barrie Mackenzie), later identified in the news media as "the hero of the riot." More importantly — to me at least — Barrie Mackenzie was also the man who had wrested control of six guard-hostages from Billy Knight (aka the Maniac in *Birdsong*), assigning them to the Inmate Protection Committee. This committee was headed by my cousin Brian Beaucage.

There were also plenty of similarities between Roger Caron and Gregory Bell. Bell was allegedly born in 1933 in rural Scotland and Roger Caron was born 1938 to a large, impoverished French-Canadian Catholic family in Cornwall, Ontario. Despite Bell's contention that his narrator Dandy was an "outsider...a novice...an amateur " and his objection to the judge that his was a "first offence," subsequent news reports indicated both Bell and Caron had been in and out of jail since they were in their teens.

They had also been committing similar kinds of crimes. Although it defies common sense, this meant they were housed together on the upper tiers of Cell Block B, mostly with inmates who formed the hard core of prison society, the aggressive personalities: the bank robbers and assault types. The aggressive personalities tended to be trouble starters and escape risks. Prison psychiatrist Dr. George C. Scott observed that when a riot broke out, ring leaders would emerge from this group of offenders.[iii]

A larger circle of thieves and robbers stood immediate to this core, Gregory Bell and Roger Caron among them, all in Cell Block B. Judging by the known crimes they had committed to date, psychiatrists such as Scott probably would have classed both Bell and Caron as sneaks or passive-aggressive personalities, small time pros who prided themselves on knowing their way around the prison. In fact, Roger Caron was sneaking around when his own lawyer actually visited the prison during the riot:

> For the short duration of Professor Morton's visit, I
> was busy exploring the darkest recesses of the attics in
> C and D blocks. January (Caron's sidekick) and I were
> still trying to get at that coffee stash inside the hobby
> craft area, only this time, from a little higher up. Thus it
> was that I missed out on my lawyer's visit to the dome area.[iv]

Despite the similarities in the basic personality types of these two fast talking, uneducated but highly verbal and well-read individuals who would later write books about their experiences, there were also subtle differences.

For one thing, although he hid behind an "alias within an alias," Gregory Bell had a minor, but starring role in the 1971 Kingston Penitentiary Riot. Low- keyed and rarely identified, he served intermittently on the Inmate Committee which ferried the prisoners' demands to the outside world. In his fictionalized account of these events, Bell's narrator Dandy Maclean claimed to be doing this so he could provide an eyewitness account of the riot. It was difficult to overlook his hero worship of Merry Thomas/Barrie McKenzie, though.

Years ago I had photocopied all the *Kingston Whig-Standard's* coverage of the 1971 Kingston Penitentiary Riot. In spite of the the heroism of inmate Barrie McKenzie, two inmate committees and a Citizen Committee of several learned men, this riot culminated in the deaths of two 'undesirables.' Thirteen inmates, including my cousin, Brian Beaucage were subsequently charged in these murders. Although newspapers are only as good as their managers and their reporters, my assumption was that the Kingston *Whig-Standard's* coverage of a tumultuous event on their own turf would be as complete as possible, but I was wrong. When my library acquired the *Toronto Star* database *Pages of the Past,* I was suddenly able to read complete news stories as far back as 1898 with relative ease. I read the coverage of my cousin's 1968 manslaughter trial first when he was just twenty-one and noted his guilt did not seem to be a sensationalist, foregone conclusion. This difference in the *Star's* and the *Whig's* coverage of the same events, prompted me to look at the *Star's* coverage of the Kingston Penitentiary Riot as well. That's where I finally found a more complete list of the men who had served on the Inmate Committee during the Riot:

- Emmanuel Lester, 47, of Toronto, serving four years for possession of stolen property;
- William "Billy" Knight of Kingston and Dresden, Ontario, serving ten years for breaking and entering and parole violation;
- Ralph Lundrigen; (no further details supplied);
- Norman McCaud, 38, of Toronto, serving four years for possession of counterfeit money;
- Barrie McKenzie, 27, of Hamilton, serving fifteen years for robbery.[v]

Additional articles would eventually identify Emmanuel Lester as an American millionaire, Billy Knight as "the inmate who started the riot and got off scot-free" and Barrie McKenzie as the hero who saved the hostage-guards, but there was no information about the other committee members. The only names I didn't recognize were Ralph Lundrigen's and Norman McCaud's, mainly because neither man had made it into in the *Kingston-Whig Standard* when they covered the riot. As Roger Caron was largely dependent on newspaper accounts to flesh out his ten year old memories, this may also explain why there are only a few references to these men in his book *Bingo!*

Norman McCaud's name caught my attention immediately, because it sounded as Scottish like *Birdsong*'s narrator, Dandy Maclean's. Estimating that McCaud had probably committed his first crime about 1955, I fed his uncommon surname (McCaud/MacCaud) into *the Toronto Star Pages of the Past* at five year intervals.

Eventually, I also researched the *Globe and Mail* and filled in more gaps.

This is a resume of his criminal career in North America (I know little of what he was doing in Dublin, Ireland where he lived from 1972-1985), punctuated with a number of characteristics matching those of Bell's fictionalized narrator Dandy Maclean. Every article, unless otherwise noted, was found in the *Toronto Star*:

- Kingston, April, 16, 1951, p.14 : "Given One Year, Like Highwayman of Old, Norman D. MacCaud, 18, of Toronto…;"
- Toronto, April 8, 1952, p.9:" Girl Terrified, Car Chased at 85 MPH, Driver, 19, Held;"
- Toronto, April 16, 1952, p.3:" On Parole, Nabbed with Stolen Auto." [vi]
- Toronto, August 11, 1956, p.1-2:" Fugitive Car Rams Detective Amid Gunfire, Norman MacCaud, alias John Sullivan…" [vii]
- Montreal, April 11, 1957, p.16: "Toronto Man Suspect in Supermarket Theft." "A man sought by Kingston and Toronto police in connection with robberies involving about $50,000 was arrested yesterday at the wheel of a car reported used in $25,000 supermarket robbery in Kingston...Police identified him as Norman McCaud, 25...they said he used the alias of Donald Goud;"
- Kingston, June 14-15, 1957, "Gets Seven Years in $27,187 Holdup."
- Kingston, September 13, 1957, p.4: "7 Years on Robbery Wounding Charge." Raymond O'Hare and Raymond McCaud both received seven years on charges of breaking into shops in Toronto and the armed robbery of the Kingston Loblaws store when $27,000 was stolen;
- Montreal, December 11, 1957, p.40: "Jailed Five Years in $420,000 Thefts." Norman McCaud, 24, of Toronto, pleaded guilty to charges of fraud and robbery involving cash and gold worth more than $20,000 and airlines rebate slips worth $400,000. McCaud was traced to Vancouver and arrested following the burglary and safe cracking there. His five year term was to run concurrent with the seven year term he was already serving at Portsmouth penitentiary, Kingston;
- Toronto, August 25, 1960, p. 20: mention in Scott Young's column that he'd had a piece accepted for the September edition of *The Diamond*, published at Collins Bay Penitentiary by editor Norman MacCaud;

- Toronto, June 4, 1963, p. 3 "Accused Ask Court for Extra Slumber." Three men charged with 106 counts of fraud... asked Magistrate Donald Graham yesterday to arrange for them to sleep later at the Don Jail... [viii]
- Toronto, February 11, 1964, p.33:" Tapped Victim's Phone: Operated Phony Cheque Ring Convict Trio on 25 Counts." Norman McCaud, 30, of Victoria Park Ave. got the stiffest sentence...10 years... Judge F.J. MacRae called him the ringleader of "this nefarious scheme" involving conspiracy to commit forgery, fraud and wiretapping. (McCaud is already serving tim .for breaking parole.) When McCaud protested his sentence, the judge snapped, "With your record, you don't seem to learn."All three accused admitted records involving crimes of violence. (see also "3 ex-Convicts in Forgery Ring Sent to Prison," *Globe and Mail*, February 12, 1964, p.5);
- Toronto (Don Jail), Jul 25, 1964: "Appeal Made to Law Society: Prisoners Ask for Aid to Get Free Evidence Transcripts" (*Globe and Mail*,p.1.);
- Toronto, September 23, 1964, p.50: "Pleads His Own Case Convict Saves $3,000. A 31-year-old Toronto convict yesterday won a rare fight to have the public pay for part of his appeal. The Ontario court of appeal...agreed with Norman McCaud's claim that he could not proceed with his appeal case until he had a transcript of evidence at his trial;
- Toronto, November 28, 1964, p.17: "Pleads Own Case But Stays in Cell." A convicted forger failed yesterday in his attempt to talk his way out of jail...Ontario Court Justice J.M. King said it would be premature to rule on Norman McCaud's motion that he was illegally arrested for violation of parole in May, 1963...In his judgment, Mr. Justice King complimented McCaud on his representation and emphasized he was not ruling on the 'substance' of his argument. (see also "Prisoner Fails in Presentation of Legal Motion," *Globe and Mail*, November 28, 1964, p.5;

- Toronto, March 23, 1965, p.29: "Printer Serving Conspiracy Sentence Uses Shelf of Books Arguing Appeal." Norman McCaud of Victoria Park Rd., who arrived in court under guard from Don Jail, stood in front of a six-foot shelf of law books and plucked volume after volume to back up his argument that the trial jury did not legally find him guilty...(although) fingerprints of McCaud were found on a roll of cheque forms (in a Bond St. office rented under a phony name for a 'snow shoveling business'). McCaud, 34, a fast talker, said he had read up on his case thoroughly and "I can't possibly be wrong...I'm in a terrible position, I know I'm not learned. All I know is what I read;"
- Toronto, March 24, 1965: "Printer Gets Praise And 3 Years." Norman McCaud...was told, "You could have become a successful lawyer" (after he argued more than four hours, starting with his conviction for auto theft when he was 18). But his conviction for conspiracy to defraud was upheld. Chief Justice Dana Porter ruled he must serve his 10 years in addition to three years of an earlier 10-year term on McCaud had been paroled. (see also "Stacks of Notes, 55 Law Books: Prisoner Loses After Arguing Own Appeal"; "Case Shows Limits of Appeal Court Power When Evidence, Jury Charge Properly Put," and "A High Moment in Justice;"[ix]
- Ottawa, May 21, 1965: "2 Toronto Men Denied Appeal;"
- Kingston, August 8, 1968, "Prisoner Wants Look at Internal Rules;" [x]
- Osgoode Hall, Toronto, November 18, 1968: re Norman MacCaud and Commissioner of Penitentiary and MacCaud's appeal to review disciplinary measures taken against him; [xi]
- Kingston, May 16, 1969, p. 67: "He Hit the Books and Cut Jail Time." Norman McCaud's indefatigable pursuit of legal knowledge in books of the prison libraries paid off yesterday. Mr. Justice N.C Fraser ruled at Osgoode Hall that, as McCaud claimed, federal authorities had indeed incorrectly counted the years left in McCaud's latest sentence. He ordered McCaud freed at once. McCaud was released from the medium-security prison at Joyceville, north of Kingston, at 5:30 p.m. The 36-year-old Torontonian had been in jail almost continuously for 12 years except for 17 months of parole... (In fact, these months were not exactly crime free. On June 11, 1970, Norman McCaud flew into Buffalo, New York and shot mobster Gino Albini.) [xii]
- Kingston, May 15, 1971, "OPP Top Investigators Probe Charge of Beatings;" [xiii]
- Napanee, June 4, 1971, "Prison Guards Submit Pleas of Not Guilty," p.27;

- Napanee, December 11, 1971, "Five Witnesses Give Similar Testimony: Gauntlet Description Repeated at Millhaven Guards' Trial;" [xiv]
- Kingston, December 30, 1971, "Given Leave, 6 Prisoners are Overdue," p.1;
- Buffalo, New York, February 2, 1972: "Fled While on Christmas leave, U.S. Provides Right to Choose Country: McCaud Cites Fear of Persecution in Canada, Wins Plea to be Deported to Ireland Instead." McCaud had entered the US illegally, so they decided to deport him to the country of his choice. US authorities were told that while in prison in 1970, somebody had acquired an Irish passport on his behalf, based on the fact that his father was a foundling in Ireland and this gave him dual citizenship. US authorities also heard that McCaud objected to being deported to Canada because the government had knowledge of his sympathies to the FLQ;
- Napanee, February 23, 1972: "McCaud Absent, Jurors Acquit Prison Guards." Three Millhaven Penitentiary guards were acquitted of assaulting a prisoner because he was in jail in Buffalo, New York. The guards were found not guilty because McCaud, the Crown's did not appear. He failed to return to Joyceville Institute farm after being given a six day pass to visit his mother in Toronto;[xv]
- Osgoode Hall, Toronto, July 10, July 11 and November 3, 1975, Untitled proceedings Regina v Norman D. MacCaud: Appeal by Norman Douglas MacCaud from order of Madame Justice Van Camp at Kingston, Sept. 26, 1975, dismissing his application for writ of habeas corpus and for his discharge from Collins Bay Institution. Appellant in person. C. Scullion for Crown Appeal dismissed;.[xvi]
- Dublin, Ireland, On 21 December 1987, Meehan, Kavanagh, Paddy Shanahan and Canadian-national Norman McCaud pulled a daring daylight robbery from the Allied Irish Bank on Grafton Street, Dublin. McCaud was a Mafia hit man… on the run … [xvii]

However, since he wasn't officially charged with Albini's murder until 1980, a parole violation most likely explains why he is was back in prison in April 1971 when the riot broke out.

Rereading Roger Caron's *Bingo!* also yielded a few small, but significant references to Norm McCaud. Hampered by the lack of information about McCaud in the Kingston Whig-Standard's coverage of the riot, Caron had briefly described him as a 38-year-old counterfeiter, serving a long term.[xviii]

According to Caron, Norm McCaud was definitely Barrie McKenzie's right hand man, though. Also, on the few occasions when McCaud did speak, his was the voice of calm reason.

In summary,

- Gregory Bell's first person narrator, Dandy Maclean and career criminal Norm McCaud both had Scottish names;
- both Dandy's fictional crimes and Norm's known crimes were similar;
- both Dandy and Norm served on the Inmate Committee during the 1971 Kingston Penitentiary Riot;:
- Dandy/Norm was Merry/Barrie's right hand man,
- both *Birdsong*'s author and the man who spent his youth in jail were well-read, highly verbal men with journalistic skills who could write a book

Yes, Judge McRae may have been correct in his assessment that Norm McCaud could have been a successful lawyer, but he also could have been a writer and he was.

Judge McRae also hit the nail on the head about McCaud's wasted potential. I would like to end this piece by writing about the redemptive power of literature, but I can't. I would like to say Norm McCaud's criminal activities were just a side line and that as he grew older, he drifted away from his life of crime, but he didn't.

I would also to know why, but I don't.

Except that when he was 13-years-old, he witnessed the murderer of cabbie Alfred Reddish fleeing the scene in west-end Toronto. Was this enough to set a gifted Bloor Collegiate student on a life of crime?

Norm McCaud eventually got a long break from jail, though. As far I can determined, he lived in the United Kingdom, possibly south of Dublin, Ireland, in Ashbourne from 1972-1985. This is almost certainly where he found the time to write a fictional account of his involvement in the 1971 Kingston Penitentiary Riot. His account may have been fictionalized to protect his friends, but it was also fictionalized because Norm McCaud had good reason for not wanting to be extradited back to Buffalo, New York where he was wanted for the 1970 murder of a mobster.

When Norm McCaud fled to the United States and in 1972 on a Christmas leave pass from Joyceville Penitentiary near Kingston and was deported to Ireland at his own request, he had become one of Canada's eight most wanted men. (*Toronto Star*, July 27, 1979)

Norman Douglas MacCaud almost certainly earned his keep in the United Kingdom through crime. Some say he was a bank robber and that he imported uncut heroin from France and Italy, through Canada to Buffalo and distributed heroin to major American cities.

Others say he was a hit man.

By the time the *Toronto Star* published "The Line-Up: Our Most Wanted Men on March 24, 1980," he had been charged him with the 1970 murder of mobster Gino Albini in Buffalo, New York: "Norman Douglas McCaud, 47, wanted by the Ontario Provincial Police for murder. With brown eyes and brown hair, McCaud is considered armed and dangerous." A photo of a balding, middle-aged man accompanied these words.

Norm McCaud evidently had some spare time, though, for it was in Ireland that he got a sabbatical to write his book.

Birdsong was released by the London publishing house of Robert Hale Ltd in 1983, none too soon, since CanLit darling Roger Caron's book was also in the making. McCaud's publishers either didn't know or didn't care if he was using an alias. I haven't been able to determine if the book was reviewed in the United Kingdom. It was not reviewed here and certainly no comparisons were made to *Birdsong* when Roger Caron's highly touted *Bingo! Four Days in Hell* was published two years later in Scarborough, Ontario by Methuen.

Although the key events of the Riot are faithfully portrayed in both books – the prison conditions leading up to the Riot, the spontaneous combustion of the takeover, the hostage-taking of the six guards, the formation of the various committees in the desperate hope of adverting disaster, the torture of fourteen men chained to a dome-like bell and the murder of the two child molesters -- *Birdsong* and *Bingo!* are clearly the accounts of two independent writers with quite different styles.

In adherence to the inmates' code of silence, Bell/McCaud carefully obscured the identity of all his friends and changed the ending of the story, while Caron rendered his fellow inmates as faithfully as possible, relying mostly on cribbed newspaper accounts.

Both men presented themselves as charitably as possible in their books: Bell/McCaud was a loner, a low man on the totem pole who had pulled a long sentence for a 'first' crime and Caron was just a merry Robin Hood, liberating whatever he could while the riot raged. Like his alter ego Dandy MacLean, McCaud was a member of the Inmate Committee, but only because he felt compelled to help his hero Barrie MacKenzie and he knew a good story when he smelled one.

As for Roger Caron, even taking notes about the riot was probably the furthest thing from his mind. He was too busy making use of a wonderful opportunity to loot and plunder. The rest of the rioters might be cowering in their cages or high on bennies and home-made brew, but freedom was so intoxicating, he didn't need drugs or alcohol.

Like their fellow inmates, McCaud and Caron were basically indifferent to what was happening to the men tortured in the dome. They knew the value of protecting the hostage guards at all costs; they knew the value of child molesters in Kingston Penitentiary and society at large.

****

When I began my search to find out the true identity of *Birdsong's* author Gregory Bell, I wanted to ask him if he remembered my cousin, that's all. I also hoped that McCaud would verify my cousin's version of the events of the riot.

My cousin Brian had accepted being a somewhat reluctant leader, but he couldn't accept being labeled a murderer for crimes he hadn't committed.

Both my cousin and his lawyers had always claimed he was the head of the Inmate Police Force who kept the six guards who had been taken hostage during 1971 Kingston Penitentiary Riot from harm. There were several attempts on the guards' lives, but they were all eventually released unharmed.

My cousin always maintained that this onerous duty had kept him too sleepless and too busy to participate in the torture of the "undesirables." Perhaps he also thought his high profile in the riot would protect him. But the words he wrote me in 1973 have proved prophetic:

> The last thing the whole world heard about me in that court room was crown evidence. That's what they'll remember the longest. Regardless of truth and lies. People think I got away with murder—literally.

Still looking for Norm McCaud, I went back to the *Toronto Star Pages of the Past* database and fed his name into the search engine long past 1985 when Ireland extradited a reputed mob boss born to the United States:

> "Ireland Extraditing Reputed Mob Boss Born in Toronto," Dublin, March 28, 1985, p.13.
> An Irish court yesterday ordered a reputed organized crime figure born in Toronto extradited to the United States to face charges of murder and drug trafficking. Norman Douglas McCaud, 52, who has been living in Ireland since the late 1970s now has 15 days in which to appeal...the murder charge (resulted) after (Gino) Albini approached McCaud and his partners for his cut (in a suburban Buffalo supermarket robbery) and they agreed to meet him and then shot him to death.

Norman Douglas MacCaud (sic) was tried and incarcerated in Buffalo, New York for the murder of Gino Albini, but this was something I only found out later. The *Toronto Star's* coverage did not extend to the Buffalo news.

I'm not sure where Norm McCaud spent the next few years after he got out jail in Buffalo in 1989, but my search for him abruptly ended when I came across an article dated February 20, 1993:

> "Police Probe Death of Reputed Mobster Found Frozen in Car." The *Star* reported that police were "investigating the death of a reputed mobster who was found frozen in a station wagon that had several parking tickets on it. Norman McCaud, 60, extradited from Ireland in the slaying of a Buffalo man in 1970, was found dead in the back seat of a friend's station wagon. The car had been on Logan Ave. near Queen St. for at least five days...
> "He was a dangerous, double-dealing robber and fraud artist...a violent man with definite mob connections," said a retired Metro staff inspector who asked his name not be used.

And so ended my quest for a man I never knew and perhaps am better off never having known, although all I felt was regret when I realized he was already dead and that he had in fact been dead when I found his book *Birdsong* in 1993.

If the *Toronto Star* reported the results of the autopsy on Norman McCaud's frozen remains, I couldn't find them. Readers were left to imagine that an aging con like McCaud was killed by a double-crossing Mafia hit man.

A small obituary published on February 24, probably placed by the Humprey Funeral Home, revealed Norman Douglas MacCaud, beloved son of Mary and the late Douglas MacCaud[xix], was survived by his unnamed wife. An only child himself, he'd had no children.

Turning to the *Virtual News* database, I was rewarded with this article from the (Waterloo) *Record* on February 22, 1993:

> A man with a long criminal record found frozen in the back seat of a parked car on east-end street in died of heart failure, an autopsy has found. Norman McCaud, 60, of Toronto died of heart failure, police said Saturday. Det. Scott Gilbert said police are still trying to trace the last steps of McCaud before he was discovered...Gilbert said the car was parked on the street either late Feb. 9 or early Feb.10, but don't know why McCaud was in that neighborhood.

The police may not have known why McCaud was in that neighborhood, but I could guess. Norman McCaud may have been a lot of things: an ex-printer, a bibliophile, a writer, a jail-house lawyer, a counterfeiter, a drug trafficker, a murderer and all those horrible things the unidentified inspector stated, but he was also a Toronto boy who came home to die.

--END--

<h2 style="text-align:center">ENDNOTES</h2>

[i] Roger Caron, *Bingo! Four Days in Hell*, Methuen: Agincourt, Ontario, p. 113.

[ii] Ibid, p.125

[iii] George D. Scott M.D. with Bill Trent, *Inmate: The Casebook Revelations of a Canadian Penitentiary Psychiatrist*, Optimum Publishing Int.: Montreal, Quebec, 1982, p.47.

[iv] Roger Caron, *Bingo! Four Days in Hell*, Methuen Publications: Agincourt, Ontario, 1985, p.163.

[v] Newspaper photos usually show four to six people on the Inmate Committee: chief spokesman Emmanuel Lester, 47, of Toronto, serving four years for

possession of stolen property (no obvious counterpart on Bell's Inmate Committee in *Birdsong*, thought his physical description matches Bell's antagonist Emmanuel Strain); Charles W. Saunders, 23 of Chatham and North Bay, serving five years for robbery with threat of violence (no obvious counterpart in Birdsong, although Caron claimed in *Bingo!* that Saunders was a staunch supporter of Billy Knight (p.104)); William "Billy" Knight of Kingston and Dresden, Ontario, serving 10 years for breaking and entering and parole violation (a k a Manny the Maniac, *Birdsong*, Bell's villain, an arsonist who should have been in an insane asylum); Ralph Lundrigen (no obvious counterpart in *Birdsong*, but Caron identifies him in *Bingo!* as a male inmate nurse, once one of the toughest and strongest cons in the joint, but a middle-aged lifer now, "most of his fire gone" (p.145)); Norman McCaud, 38, of Toronto, variously reported as serving four years for possession of counterfeit money or ten years for forgery (a k a Dandy Maclean in *Birdsong*) and Barrie McKenzie, 27, of Hamilton, serving 15 years for robbery (aka Meredith "Merry" Thomas, *Birdsong*'s hero).

[vi] See also *the Globe and Mail*, April 9, 1952, p.5.

[vii] See also "In Path of Car, Detective Thrown Over Fence," *the Globe and Mail*, August 13, 1956, p.5);

[viii] *Globe and Mail*, June 4, 1963, p.5);

[ix] Ibid, March 24, 1965, p.5; "April 5, 1965; April 8, 1965, p. 6);

[x] Ibid, August 8, 1968

[xi] Ibid, November 18, 1968, p.35.

[xii] See also *Globe and Mail*, May 16, 1969, p.5;

[xiii]Ibid, May 15, 1971, p.10.

[xiv] Ibid, December 11, 1971, p.10.

[xv] Ibid, February 23, 1972.

[xvi] Ibid, Untitled court proceedings from Osgoode, *Globe and Mail*, July 10, July 11 and November 3, 1975, p.59.

[xvii]Paul Williams, *Badfellas*, Penguin, 2011.

[xviii] *Bingo!*, p.167.

[xix] Norm's father, Norman Douglas MacCaud had died Dec 24, 1963, East General Hospital, Toronto. Resided 105 Gainsborough Rd., husband of Mary Watson and father of Norman (*Toronto Daily Star*, Dec 26, 1963: 36). Norm's mother, Mary Henderson Watson, died 29 Aug 1998, age 86 at the Thompson House in Toronto. Wife of the late Douglas T. MacCaud, mother of the late Norman Douglas MacCaud, sister of the late Stuart, John, Robert Watson and Elizabeth (Elsie) Chipman. Survived by sister Sarah (Sadie) Windsor. (*Toronto Star*, 31 Aug 1998: C6)

www.ingramcontent.com/pod-product-compliance
Lightning Source LLC
Chambersburg PA
CBHW060607030426
42337CB00019B/3642